OUR SOLAR SYSTEM
MERCURY
THE FASTEST PLANET

by Mari Schuh

pogo

Ideas for Parents and Teachers

Pogo Books let children practice reading informational text while introducing them to nonfiction features such as headings, labels, sidebars, maps, and diagrams, as well as a table of contents, glossary, and index.

Carefully leveled text with a strong photo match offers early fluent readers the support they need to succeed.

Before Reading

- "Walk" through the book and point out the various nonfiction features. Ask the student what purpose each feature serves.
- Look at the glossary together. Read and discuss the words.

Read the Book

- Have the child read the book independently.
- Invite him or her to list questions that arise from reading.

After Reading

- Discuss the child's questions. Talk about how he or she might find answers to those questions.
- Prompt the child to think more. Ask: Mercury's surface has many craters. How did these craters form?

Pogo Books are published by Jump!
5357 Penn Avenue South
Minneapolis, MN 55419
www.jumplibrary.com

Library of Congress Cataloging-in-Publication Data

Names: Schuh, Mari C., 1975– author.
Title: Mercury : the fastest planet / by Mari Schuh.
Description: Minneapolis, MN: Jump!, Inc., [2023]
Series: Our solar system | Includes index.
Audience: Ages 7-10
Identifiers: LCCN 2022029576 (print)
LCCN 2022029577 (ebook)
ISBN 9798885243551 (hardcover)
ISBN 9798885243568 (paperback)
ISBN 9798885243575 (ebook)
Subjects: LCSH: Mercury (Planet)–Juvenile literature.
Classification: LCC QB611 .S48 2023 (print)
LCC QB611 (ebook)
DDC 523.41–dc23/eng20220917
LC record available at https://lccn.loc.gov/2022029576
LC ebook record available at https://lccn.loc.gov/2022029577

Editor: Jenna Gleisner
Designer: Emma Bersie

Photo Credits: Markik/Shutterstock, cover (background); Dotted Yeti/Shutterstock, cover (Mercury); NASA/ Johns Hopkins University Applied Physics Laboratory/ Carnegie Institution of Washington, 1, 3, 13, 14-15, 17; ixpert/Shutterstock, 4 (Earth); Chones/Shutterstock, 4 (Moon); dotted zebra/Alamy, 5 (Mercury); Klever_ok/ Shutterstock, 5 (background); Lauritta/Shutterstock, 6-7; Shutterstock, 8-9; alexaldo/Shutterstock, 10-11; Mopic/ Shutterstock, 12; NASA Image Collection/Alamy, 16; 3Dsculptor/Shutterstock, 18-19; Kirill Cherezov/Alamy, 20-21 (Mercury); Klanarong Chitmung/Shutterstock, 20-21 (background); Vadim Sadovski/Shutterstock, 23.

Printed in the United States of America at Corporate Graphics in North Mankato, Minnesota.

For Paige

TABLE OF CONTENTS

CHAPTER 1

CLOSE TO THE SUN

Have you ever looked at Earth's Moon? Maybe you have seen it through a **telescope**. Did you see its **craters**?

crater

Earth's Moon

The **planet** Mercury looks a lot like the Moon. It also has craters.

Mercury

Where do the craters come from? **Meteorites** hit Mercury. They cause the large holes.

meteorite

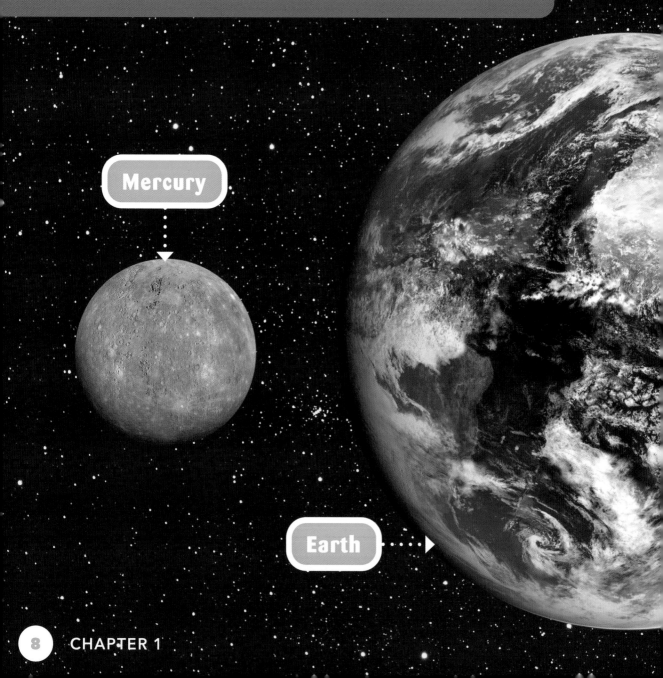

Mercury is the smallest planet in our **solar system**. It could fit inside Earth at least 18 times!

Mercury

Earth

TAKE A LOOK!

Mercury is closer to the Sun than any other planet. Take a look!

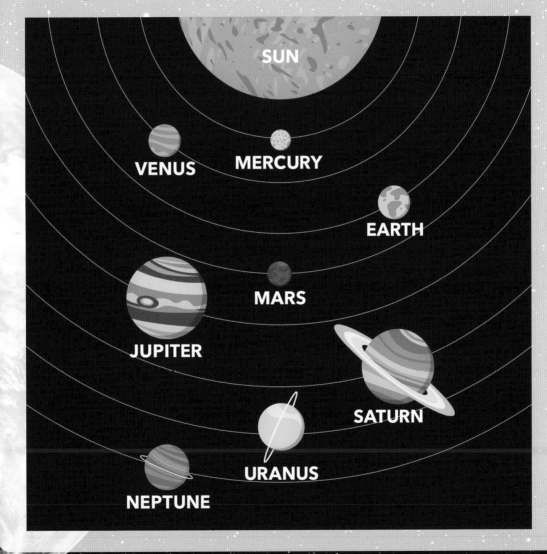

SUN

VENUS   MERCURY

EARTH

JUPITER   MARS

SATURN

URANUS

NEPTUNE

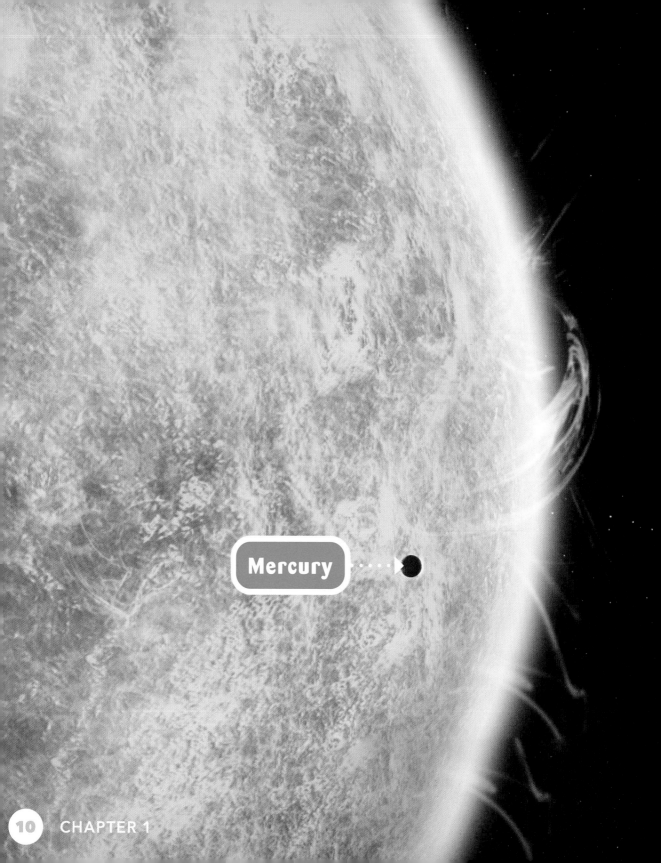

Mercury

All planets **orbit** the Sun. Mercury orbits faster than the other planets. Why? It is closest to the Sun. The distance it has to travel is shorter.

The Sun's **gravity** strongly pulls on Mercury. Stronger gravity also makes a planet travel faster.

DID YOU KNOW?

One full orbit around the Sun is one year. One year for Earth is 365 days. One year for Mercury is 88 Earth days.

CHAPTER 2

ALL ABOUT MERCURY

Because Mercury is so close to the Sun, it can be very hot. How hot? Temperatures can be 800 degrees Fahrenheit (430 degrees Celsius)!

Nights can be very cold. Why? Mercury has a very thin **atmosphere**. It does not have clouds or thick layers of gases to hold in heat.

cliff ····▶

Mercury's crust is rocky. Its surface is dry. Long, steep cliffs are found on parts of Mercury. Other parts are flat.

TAKE A LOOK!

What are Mercury's layers? Take a look!

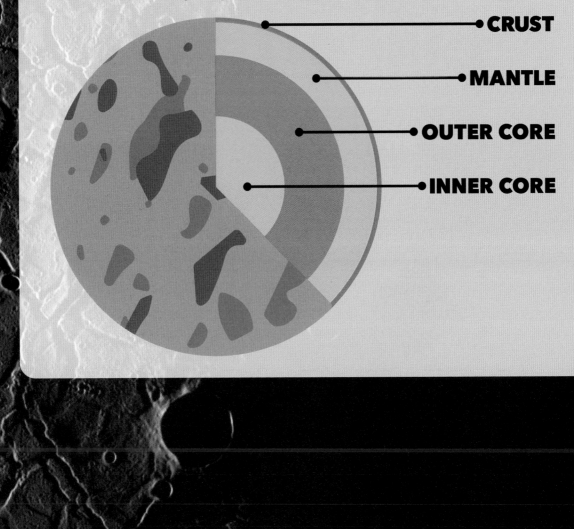

- CRUST
- MANTLE
- OUTER CORE
- INNER CORE

CHAPTER 3

AMAZING DISCOVERIES

In 1974, the **spacecraft** *Mariner 10* made history. Why? It became the first spacecraft to visit Mercury. It flew by Mercury three times. It studied the planet.

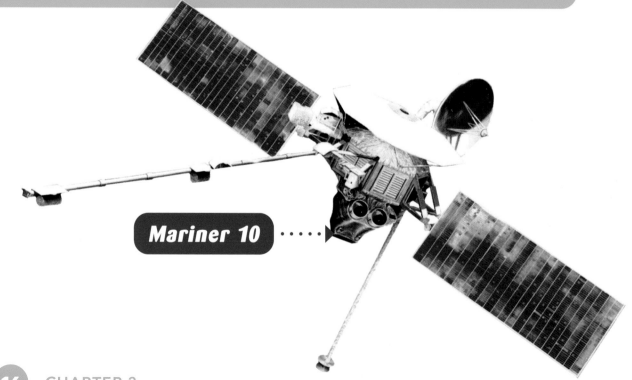

Mariner 10

Mariner 10 took more than 2,700 photos of Mercury. The photos showed about half of Mercury's surface. *Mariner 10* also studied the planet's atmosphere and surface.

The spacecraft *Messenger* was the first to orbit Mercury. It orbited the planet from 2011 to 2015. It studied Mercury's surface. *Messenger* also helped scientists learn more about Mercury's **core**. It is solid. It is much bigger than scientists thought.

DID YOU KNOW?

Mercury does not have any moons. Neither does Venus. They are the only two planets in our solar system without moons.

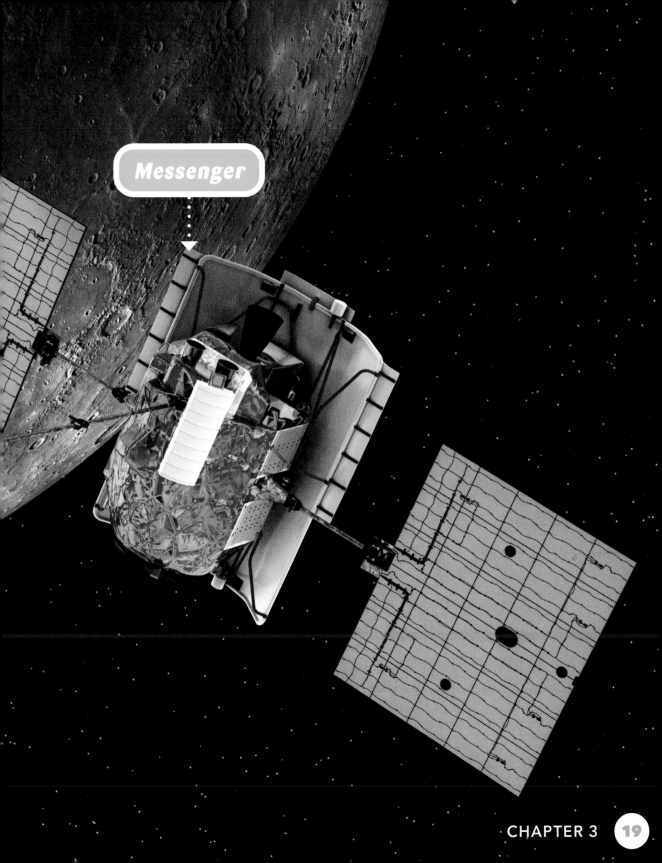

Messenger

In 2021, *BepiColombo* flew by Mercury for the first time. It is named after Italian Professor Giuseppe "Bepi" Colombo. The spacecraft will fly by Mercury five more times and orbit it. Scientists hope to learn more about how Mercury formed.

Mercury is an amazing planet. What more would you like to discover about it?

DID YOU KNOW?

Galileo Galilei was an **astronomer**. So was Thomas Harriot. They made history in 1631. Why? They were the first to see Mercury with a telescope.

ACTIVITIES & TOOLS

MERCURY'S SURFACE

Some areas of Mercury's surface are smooth. Other areas have craters. Learn more about Mercury's surface with this fun activity!

What You Need:
- cake pan
- flour
- small marbles, rocks, or chocolate chips

❶ Put a thick layer of flour in the cake pan. Smooth the flour so it is flat and even.

❷ Find a safe, flat area outside. Put the cake pan on the ground.

❸ Drop marbles, rocks, or chocolate chips into the pan.

❹ Now carefully take the items out of the pan.

❺ Look at the flour now. Does the flour have craters? Are they different sizes? Why do you think this is?

GLOSSARY

astronomer: A scientist who studies stars, planets, and space.

atmosphere: The mixture of gases that surrounds a planet.

core: The center, most inner part of a planet.

craters: Large holes in the ground that are made when pieces of rock or metal in space crash into a planet or moon.

gravity: The force that pulls things toward the center of a planet and keeps them from floating away.

meteorites: Pieces of rock or metal in space that hit a planet or moon.

orbit: To travel in a circular path around something.

planet: A large body that orbits, or travels in circles around, the Sun.

solar system: The Sun, together with its orbiting bodies, such as the planets, their moons, and asteroids, comets, and meteors.

spacecraft: Vehicles that travel in space.

telescope: A device that uses lenses or mirrors in a long tube to make faraway objects appear bigger and closer.

INDEX

TO LEARN MORE

Finding more information is as easy as 1, 2, 3.

❶ Go to www.factsurfer.com

❷ Enter "Mercury" into the search box.

❸ Choose your book to see a list of websites.

FACT SURFER